21 ways

to make
money
speaking

Felicia Slattery, M.A., M.Ad.Ed.

Discover! BOOKS™
an Imprint of Imagine! Books™

High Point, North Carolina

21 Ways™ Series, Book 4

Published by Discover! Books™
an Imprint of Imagine! Books™
PO Box 16268, High Point, NC 27261
contact@artsimagine.com

Imagine! Books™ is an enterprise of Imagine! Studios™
Visit us online at www.artsimagine.com

ISBN 13: 978-1-937944-02-5

First Discover! Books™ printing, February 2012

Dedication

I dedicate this book to all past, current, and future students of my *Signature Speech* system for bringing in new clients. Once you start speaking in public you'll never want to stop, so I wrote this book for you and anyone who has the love of speaking and the entrepreneurial spirit to make some money doing it. Thank you for your support and your drive for success.

Without you, I have no business.

Acknowledgements

The words "thank you" seem so small in light of the wonderful support I've received in completing this book.

First to my publisher and friend, Kristen Eckstein, thank you for planting the seeds for, and offering me the opportunity to write, a short book jam-packed with all the best ways I know to make money speaking.

To my assistants, Rebekah Zobel Jones, Kristen Hamlin, and Seychelle Marasigan: Without your keeping me organized and making sure the wheels are well oiled, I don't know how I could function in my business!

To all the event planners, affiliate partners, and others who have put me on your virtual and live stages and allowed me to earn a living doing the thing I love the most, I am humbly honored and grateful to you for each opportunity.

Finally, to my family, especially my husband, Brent Parkhill, thank you for giving me space and allowing me to be who I am. I love the life we've created.

Introduction

When my publisher initially approached me about writing this book, honestly I agreed as a favor to her. She was just launching her "21 Ways" series, and, having seen me speak and having taken some of my public speaking training herself, she knew I had some valuable information to share.

The more I wrote, however, the more excited I became. The Ways in this book represent some creative, fun, and interesting ways to make money by speaking.

While some of the Ways throughout this book do not specifically address speaking on a live, or even virtual, stage, I believe that each is essential. Using the power of your voice, speaking with people and earning a living by simply talking can easily become some of the most rewarding experiences of your life—personally, professionally, and financially. It certainly has for me and I hope after reading this book, it will for you as well.

To your massive speaking success and happiness!
~*Felicia*

Keynote Speaker

Keynote speaking is where you get to be the star speaker of an event. Keynote speaking is a highly entertaining style of speaking that also delivers a meaning, message, or big-picture type of take-away for the audience. Keynote speakers, no matter their background, should provide some sort of knowledge, opinion, or insight about what's currently happening in their particular industry.

As a keynote speaker you'll be promoted on the event website, where you and your topic will often be used as a way to attract more attendees to the event. Typical keynote speaking opportunities include the following:

Opening keynote

This speaker will kick off the event and get the attendees excited about what's to come. Typically if there is an opening keynote speaker, the event runs over several days where there are likely other speakers, such as breakout session speakers (see Way 2).

Closing keynote

If you're asked to be the closing keynote speaker, you'll be ending what was likely a multi-day event and leaving the audience with their final impressions and lasting memories of that event.

After-dinner speaker

This keynote type of speech is typically much more entertainment than content-driven. Your goal: get the audience laughing and having a fun time.

Keynote speaker

If an event has just one headliner, this person is known as the keynote speaker and will present usually at a featured time where all attendees can be present.

Easy ways to transition to becoming a keynote speaker:

Be a well-respected leader in your industry

When everyone in your industry knows your name and respects your work, you become the sought-after choice for various association and conference meetings.

Be a current or former professional athlete or Olympic athlete

Take your past athletic career and translate the stories into relatable, teachable moments for your audiences.

Be a current or former politician or corporate CEO

Talk about the hot topics in politics and/or business now and relate your stories to share teachable moments with your audience.

Be a best-selling author

With the prominence that comes with having a best-selling book, often your phone will ring with speaking opportunities. Talk about highlights and material from your book. If you want to learn more about exactly how to do this, check out my SignatureSpeechForAuthors.com.

Be a motivational or general keynote speaker

Even without having the background of an athlete, politician, or business leader, you can simply prepare a motivational speech with a fabulous title and market yourself to groups where your message makes the most sense.

$ How you make money

For a keynote speech, you are paid just for showing up, delivering your best, and lending your name for advance publicity of the event. You should also ask for your travel expenses to be covered, including airfare, hotel accommodations at the event location, transport to and from the airport, and meals while you are traveling, typically paid as a per diem flat amount. The latest trend in speaking fees is to present one all-inclusive fee to the event planner so the event planner never has to worry about extra travel expenses being tacked on later. However you do it, clearly communicate all your fees.

Speaking fees vary widely, with the most prominent names garnering $50,000–$100,000 per speaking engagement. Fees for less well-known speakers usually start in the $1,000 range. Other than possibly mentioning that your books are available at the back of the room or in the event bookstore, there typically is *no* selling during this type of presentation and is in fact *highly* frowned upon.

Resources in this Way:

 SignatureSpeechForAuthors.com

Breakout Session Speaker

As a breakout session speaker you are asked to present an educational session, typically at a multi-day, multi-track type of event. Unlike *Way 1: Keynote Speaking*, where you are the star of the show, a breakout session speaker provides the informational meat-and-potatoes of any event (or beans-and-rice if you're on a budget!).

When you are a breakout session speaker, your session will likely be promoted on the event website and in the event program. You can do well if you have a specific topic or area of expertise that can help a wide variety of industries. The more general popular topics include, but are not limited to, communication, customer service, leadership, productivity, and financing.

Or you can also do well if you have a current hot topic that everyone wants to learn more about, such as social media, mobile marketing, technology advances, or emerging trends.

Regardless of the topic you select, your presentation must be something unique to have the best chance at being a breakout speaker. No one wants to hire just another "time management" speaker who is going to regurgitate the same old advice (yawn) everyone has heard a thousand times. You've got to have a hook, stand out, and be different.

If you happen to live in or near a large metro area that hosts many conferences and conventions, you could have a bit of a leg up on your competition. These days, many event planners are stretching limited funds and therefore have little to no budget for paying the travel expenses for breakout session trainers. For example, marketing yourself as an "Atlanta professional speaker" or "Boston customer service speaker" will help event planners more easily find you when they are searching your large metro area. Even if you live in a suburb or town that is not in the main city, like Kissimmee, Fla., you still should market yourself as an "Orlando-based speaker," so when an event planner searches that phrase online, you appear at the top of the rankings.

$ How you make money

As a breakout session speaker, you make money for showing up and delivering your content. Speaking fees vary widely for breakout session speakers, also sometimes called trainers. Remember that once an event planner is interested in your topic, every-thing else is negotiable. For example, you may find the $500–$800 budget the event planner originally told you about can be stretched to $1,000 or even more if you are the right fit for the event's audience. Simply asking for more can get you a higher fee. As with Way 1, other than possibly mentioning that your books are available at the back of the room or in the event bookstore, there typically is *no* sell-ing during this type of presentation and is *highly* frowned upon.

Sell Your Books

Wait—before the publishing world and my author marketing friends go wild, let me be clear. The title of this book is **not** *21 Ways to Get Richer-than-a-Rockefeller Quick*. Most authors do not make a lot of money selling their books. It's what you do after the sale.

With that caveat in place, you can definitely make money at your speaking engagements by selling your books. Last summer I was a keynote speaker at an event with a book signing for two authors and me. We all sold books and made money!

Use these tips to make money selling books while speaking:

Back-of-the-room sales

Sell your books at the back of the room. This is the easiest and most common way to make money when combining speaking and book sales. Any time you are in front of a live audience, request that the event planner have a sales table set up for you at the back of the room. Arrive early, bring an assistant to staff the table (friends or family members often don't mind helping out!), and set up a simple display.

Free book option

Offer the event planner the option for everyone in the room to get a book. Often if your book is directly related to the reason you've been invited to speak, an event planner might be willing to purchase a book for each audience member if you offer the books at a volume discount. Offer to do a book signing after speaking so audience members can get their copies of your book signed. If attendees must pay admission, suggest adding the discounted cost of the book to the event price.

The teleseminar

Hold a teleseminar specifically to sell your books. I love this option because you can make money from the comfort of your own home or office. Use a free conference call service such as FreeConferenceCall.com, or, for more bells and whistles, try my personal favorite, ProfessionalTeleseminars.com. Simply share your private conference number and PIN code with your audience, and allow them to come on the call and ask questions. You can present some content from your book, or even read an excerpt over the phone.

Talk about it

Discuss your speaking services in your book. If you're still writing your book, pepper it with stories and ideas about how you could come into a group and present your material. Remember, if you never let people know you're a speaker, how will they find out? You must continually position yourself in all your work as a person who is willing to speak to groups of all sizes, both on a live stage or virtually. The more happy readers of your book, the more paid opportunities you'll get to speak.

The magic combination

Combine selling your book while speaking at another one of the places suggested throughout the rest of this book. See Ways 4, 6, 8, 9, 10, 11, 12, 14, 18, and 21 for details and then simply add selling your book to any of the other ways and—BOOM!—instant multiple streams of income from one speaking opportunity.

Don't have a book? My publisher Kristen Eckstein, *The Ultimate Book Coach*, has put together a free webinar outlining how she wrote a nonfiction book in 3 1/2 days and how you can, too. Grab it at BooksForSpeakers.com.

Resources in this Way:

 FreeConferenceCall.com

 ProfessionalTeleseminars.com

 BooksForSpeakers.com

Sell from the Stage

Selling from the stage. Speaking from the platform. Selling from the platform. These are several names describing same thing: As a speaker you get paid for selling products and services during your presentation.

Some folks who make money selling from the stage tend to be less polished in their speaking techniques, and more gifted at selling their content. The best, including those who make tens of thousands of dollars selling from the platform, are as skilled in their presentation style as they are in their ability to sell.

What can you sell? Almost anything related to your business, including your book(s) (see Way 3); consulting services; a teleseminar or webinar series you teach live; a teleseminar or webinar series you've taught previously that can be accessed online; packaged DVD or CD sets with manuals, checklists, transcripts, etc.; access to a membership program; one- or multi-day live workshops, in-depth trainings, or seminars; and mastermind groups, both live and virtual.

$ How you make money

If you're not familiar with this option, you may be shocked. For those of us selling from the platform, we typically pay all of our own travel expenses to what are usually multi-day events. Occasionally an event host will plan a speakers' dinner; include a meal for all participants, speakers included; or host a VIP cocktail party, so you might get a free meal.

If you're selling from the stage, you are not paid to show up. You make your money strictly by selling. Part of the deal is that the event host will require you to split your earnings from the event with them. At first glance this may not sound fair, especially with you paying your own way and not getting paid a speaking fee. Yet when you take into account the fact the event host did all the marketing work to put your ideal audience into the seats (known affectionately in the industry as "putting butts in seats"), did all the planning for the event, dealt with the hotel, and took a financial risk in terms of hotel minimums and food costs, and all you needed to do is show up and speak? That's not too bad.

Count on your costs for everything, including your prep time, travel costs, and three-part carbonless order forms for everyone in the room to be around $1,000. Most event hosts will ask for around 50 percent of your sales. So that means you need to sell at least $2,000 of your products or services to break even. For that reason, most speakers create bundled packages that can only be purchased at that specific event, providing a compelling reason for audience members to purchase right then and there. Price your products accordingly, and if you're speaking to the right audience, selling what they want, and making it irresistible, you'll make great money. If you plan well and offer other products and services to those new customers you met at the event later (and, by the way, you keep 100 percent of the profits from all subsequent sales), you will continue to make more money from those new customers for years to come.

Get Consulting Gigs from the Stage

Regardless of whether you're paid to speak at a live event, as in Ways 1 and 2, or if you're selling from the stage, as in Way 4, or if you're presenting some other kind of live or virtual event as in almost all the other Ways in this book, when audience members know you offer consulting services, they will approach you to pay for your consulting services. Pepper your presentation with stories, case studies, and examples from your past consulting clients. Remember to ask for permission to use exact names from your clients, or else speak generally.

If you're not already offering consulting services, consider including that option. You can conduct consulting in any number of ways, including the following:

In person locally

This type of consulting can be conducted by the hour at your office or at a "satellite office" such as a coffee shop, restaurant, bookstore, or other public location. It's a nice touch if coffee, breakfast, or lunch is on you when the other person is paying you to be there.

Privately via phone

This consulting is billed by hour or half-hour. As a value add-on extra bonus, you could offer to record the consulting sessions for your clients so they refer back to all of your brilliant ideas. Use an upgraded service like ProfessionalTeleseminar.com so your clients can have a private web page automatically generated for immediate and ongoing access after your consulting session with very minimal set-up work from you.

Group consulting via phone

This type offers a lower price point for those who cannot afford the investment in your private services. Consider limiting the number of people in the group to encourage people to enroll quickly and to keep yourself from being overwhelmed with questions during sessions.

In person, at their location

Offer this type of consulting for an hour, half day, full day, or multiple days, depending on the issue on which you're consulting. Remember to specify in your contract or letter of agreement that your travel expenses should also be paid, or figure them into the consulting fee.

VIP days or half-days

If you work with one-on-one clients around the country or internationally, provide the option for them to escape their day-to-day business and travel to your location—either at your office or in a hotel conference room. There they will get intensive help from you with one specific area. I offer this option virtually as well through free video conferencing with Skype or Oovoo.com.

$ How you make money

When offering consulting as an option, be sure you are paid for your services in advance. In fact, according to most of the sales experts I have studied, you should request your fees immediately when the client says yes. Have a way to take credit card information over the phone on the spot, using a virtual terminal available through PayPal or another online merchant, or one of the many iPhone or iPad applications, such as Square or Innerfence. Clients should not be considered fully committed until they have committed with their cash. Once they have made that financial commitment to you, they have also made that commitment to themselves and are far less likely to cancel. Decide if your fee is hourly or flat, how you will charge for travel expenses, and determine a cancellation policy that ensures you still get paid something if they cancel at the last minute, especially if your travel expenses can't be refunded.

Resources in this Way:

 Skype.com

 Oovoo.com

 PayPal.com

 Square/Innerfence.com

Speak to Help a Charity

If you're looking for a unique way to make money as a speaker and help a worthy cause at the same time, here's a fabulous technique I learned from Tom Antion, fellow professional speaker and speaker trainer.

Contact your favorite local charity and offer to put on a paid presentation for their members. Repeat at other charities. This works well for many reasons. First, you have a ready-made audience in the supporters of the charity. Second, the charity likely has a well-oiled marketing engine in place to get the word out about your presentation. It also likely has a space to accommodate you and the audience at the charity's facility. Fourth, charities are always looking for new and unique ways to bring in more funds and will likely be amenable to your presentation. You might be able to write off the part of your fee that you donate back to the organization (check with your qualified tax advisor on the details on how to do this properly).

$ How you make money

When you contact the organization follow these steps:

Step 1

Familiarize yourself with the charity's donors or audience so you know what type of presentation will most appeal to those benefactors. Research this on the charity's website. For example, are they a specific religion, do they have a political affiliation, or do they offer services for a certain demographic? The local women's shelter might want a different type of presentation than the local chapter of Young Republicans, for example.

Step 2

Call the charity and ask to speak with the person in charge of fundraising. Present your proposal over the phone and follow up with more details in writing.

Explain you will charge an entrance fee to the event, such as $20 per ticket, and you will collect and organize all those coming to the event. Offer to split the entrance fee with the charity at 50/50.

Step 3

During the event, sell something from the stage and tell the charity you plan to split any of those sales with the event receiving 25 percent and you 75 percent.

Also sell your books at the back of the room for a discounted rate and offer the charity 10 percent of all book sales.

Step 4

After the event, continue to reach out to the audience members using a segmented contact list with more offers. Continue to donate a percentage of your proceeds from that audience back to the charity. You'll make money for years to come, the charity will continue to receive donations, and you'll increase your sales because the charity's fans will buy more knowing a portion of their funds go back to their favorite charity.

Be an Emcee

Every live event needs an energetic person to kick off the event, keep things moving and on schedule, and make sure the audience is having fun and is fully engaged. That's the job of a Master or Mistress of Ceremonies, Emcee or MC for short. Occasionally also referred to as a "come back" speaker; this is someone who gets the audience to come back to the conference room after breaks.

An emcee is valuable to an event for many reasons. First, he or she keeps the event planner or host from having to be on stage. Many event planners prefer to be in the background making things work, not on stage in front of an audience.

Second, an emcee will boost sales at the event, whether speakers are selling from the platform (see

Way 4) or not. If the event has a bookstore, for example, you as emcee can direct audience members to the bookstore before break periods, and highlight specific books or products for sale in the bookstore.

Third, the emcee keeps the event running on time by offering free giveaways to audience members for coming back to the event conference room on time after breaks. Use books donated by the speakers, T-shirts, candy, gift certificates, etc., as ethical bribes to get people back in their seats on time. Each person in his or her seat on time gets a gift or is eligible for a prize.

Fourth, the emcee can be the communicator for the event host for any announcements or changes in the event schedule.

And lastly, an emcee creates information hunger and excitement for each phase of the event including speakers, vendors, sponsors, parties, auctions, and more.

Once you are booked as emcee, you have a few steps to complete in order to make the event a success:

Step 1

Meet with the event organizer to be sure you understand her expectations and what's important to her.

Step 2

Get the event schedule in advance of the event, even if it slightly changes. Suggest areas for improvement if you see them, such as extending five-minute breaks to fifteen or twenty minutes to allow for participants to mingle and make purchases.

Step 3

If you will be introducing speakers, ask if the organizer has the speakers' introductions. If not, do your own research to get those intros or bios from the speakers' websites, or, with permission from the event organizer, contact the speakers yourself to obtain them. Practice reading the speaker introductions and any other material or scripts your event organizer sends you in advance.

Step 4

At the event, make sure you have a point person. Often the event organizer will have another meeting professional managing the details. Connect with that person to be sure everything runs smoothly.

Step 5

Remember, as an emcee, it's *not* about you. Check your ego at the door and make the event fun for the participants. Focus on the speakers, sponsors, vendors, and other stars of the show. Let your personality shine through and have a great time! When you're having fun, the audience will have fun too.

$ How you make money

As an emcee you have several options for making money:

✓ Charge a flat fee to be the event emcee.

✓ Charge a percentage of all sales at the event.

✓ Sell your books and products in the event bookstore.

✓ Connect with the other speakers to build relationships and later do joint ventures and affiliate promotions with them (see Way 14).

✓ Get a sponsor to pay for you to be emcee (see Way 19).

Conduct a Local Workshop

When you have a message to share, sharing it locally is an easy way to get quick feedback from a live audience and make money at the same time. One of my past clients regularly conducts paid local workshops, which feeds new clients into her consulting business.

Many experts and entrepreneurs often take for granted what they know, live, and breathe and assume "everybody knows that." Or they think their knowledge is "just common sense."

The litmus test: If you have specialized knowledge or have had advanced training in a particular area, field, or discipline, and people often approach you to "pick your brain" about what you know, my friend, you have saleable information people would pay to receive and understand better. Yay you!

Here are a few types of local workshops you could teach:

Sixty-minute lunch and learn

Attendees bring their own brown-bag lunches and you supply the chocolate chip cookies. They pay a small fee to attend and eat lunch while you teach.

Early morning workshop

Fitness workshops often go over well in the very early morning hours, as do business functions that allow participants to get in a little networking in addition to your workshop training.

Evening workshop

If your topic is more of a personal nature rather than business, an evening might be a good choice.

Half-day workshop

Some skills take longer to teach than others. Also, in half-day workshops participants can take the opportunity to do hands-on work with your guidance.

Full-day workshop

This workshop might be more difficult to sell if you're not already an established figure in your industry and/or local area because people will wonder if a full day is worth their time and energy away from their regular routines and other pressing matters. If you give people a reason why a full-day workshop is not only necessary but also vital, and will give them a huge return on their time investment for months or years to come, they will show up in droves.

As with anything you create and sell, keep in mind your audience's particular needs. For example, if your workshop is to teach moms of multiples how to be more organized, consider hiring a babysitting staff (a handful of responsible local teens or college kids eager to make a few quick bucks?) to take care of all the kiddos so the moms can focus.

$ How You Make Money

In my town, the local bank has meeting space free for the asking. You don't even have to be a customer of the bank! It's part of their community outreach and gives the bank an opportunity to get its brochures into the hands of the people who come in for the meeting. There are often many locations willing to share their conference room space free of charge in exchange for being mentioned in your publicity as a sponsor (more on sponsorships in Way 19) and being allowed to pass out their materials. Also try Realtors' offices, libraries, and churches. Then charge each participant a fee that is a great deal. You'll get to pocket all of that, add these folks to your marketing lists, and upsell more books, products, and services during your workshop to make even more cash. Ka-ching!

Hold Your Own National Multi-Day Event

I might not suggest this be the first thing you try right out of the gate, but I know many business owners who make running their own national events a major part of their income-producing work each year.

Before planning your own multi-day event, I suggest you first attend several similar in format to what you would like to plan yourself. There are several types of events you could run:

The "you show"

This type of event takes *a lot* of energy on your part during the event, but is also highly fulfilling because it's all you for seven to eight hours each day, plus entertaining in the evenings. Determine what topic your event will focus on; plan to teach a lot of detailed, nitty-gritty type stuff; and keep in mind that you're on stage for two to three days in a row. Your audience can be any size, from an intimate audience who perhaps paid high fees to attend, to a larger group of a couple hundred paying more moderate or even low fees to attend.

Multi-speaker platform event

You could be the event organizer and invite other speakers to join you. These speakers will sell from the stage, as discussed in detail in Way 4. Of course you also get to speak as much or as little as you like. You get to keep a large percentage of any sales the speakers make while on stage, so if you hire speakers who understand what it takes to sell with integrity from the stage and do so regularly, you can bring in mind-blowing money.

Convention-style event

If you're ready to take a big plunge, you could plan an event to suit an entire industry or segment of an industry. Vendors pay you a fee to set up in a convention hall, attendees pay to attend, sponsors pay to get in front of your attendees and get ads in the convention guide, and often you can find local speakers willing to speak for free or very nominal fees if they happen to be delivering their Signature Speech (see Way 21). Get a sponsor to pony up for a big name in the industry as your keynote speaker and main draw to the event (or be your own keynote speaker!) and you're well on your way to a big time show. Word of warning: Don't try to tackle this alone, especially if you have no major event planning experience. A professional event planner for this style event is worth her weight in gold!

Present a Webinar

The word "webinar" has an interesting history. First, waaaay before the Internet, there were plain old "seminars" and "conferences." As technology evolved, businesses began using "teleconferences" on the phone, where more than one person could participate over a long distance and from various locations. As related services evolved, soon people could use "bridge lines"—one central number everyone could call into to meet together. And now that virtual meetings take place regularly, yes, you can literally make money while working in your pajamas!

Savvy presenters quickly realized they could use those bridge lines to teach seminars on the phone, which came to be called "teleseminars." Teleseminars are still popular today, especially given that technology for teleseminars has been around longer than that for webinars, and it's user-friendly. Typically all that is required to participate is a phone and a special number and PIN code—resulting in fewer tech "issues."

"Webinars" use the same general concept of a teleseminar, but instead of connecting via the phone lines, participants and presenters connect over the Internet, using technology that allows the presenter to show images on the screen live as the call progresses.

The benefits of a webinar that go beyond what you could do with a teleseminar include:

✓ Using your voice along with carefully selected images of your choosing to reinforce your message, often adding another layer of emotion.

✓ Graphically represent a concept.

✓ Show a screen capture or share a screen live.

✓ Live polling on some services.

$ How You Make Money

Sellinar

Sell your own products or invite a guest to teach their content and sell their products to your audience. If you opt for the guest, you get to keep an affiliate commission.

Launchinar

Similar to a "sellinar," you could create a "launchinar" to present the world premiere of a new product or service, or a new book where you present a reading. During the call, offer participants an opportunity and a reason to purchase now.

Teachinar

Create a course around your area of expertise and invite participants to attend for a fee. This could be a one-time webinar or a webinar series. A fun bonus of this option is you are paid to make a product that you will sell later as a digital product instead of a live class. This is one form of "repurposing."

How long should your webinar be? The answer is up to you, and what's right for your content and purpose. I've seen webinars go as little as thirty minutes and go as long as three or more *hours*. Remember, with a webinar audience members are pretty much tied to their computer screens to be able to fully participate and get the full webinar experience. In my personal opinion, if your webinar goes longer than ninety minutes, I've observed participants begin to experience something I'll call "webinar fatigue"—they're tired of sitting still, need a break and begin to resent you for making them feel like they might miss something important if they disconnect. Some may argue therein lies an element of control, but I'd counter that with a simple question: Do you want your audience to resent you?

WAY **11**

Virtual Workshop

Invite guests to join you for a webinar or teleseminar and have them work through activities, tasks, or steps that will deliver some value to them by the end of the workshop. I saw this done well by one of my earliest online mentors, Jeff Herring, who teaches article marketing. Here's how he ran his call using a webinar service (see Way 10). You can follow this model for your own workshop and make money as he did:

Step 1

Welcome participants and introduce the call. Right after the welcome, share your personal story—called the ETR or "earn the right" story—so people know why they should listen to you.

Step 2

Invite the participants to interact with you and explain how they can do so.

Step 3

Present content: definitions and descriptions.

Step 4

Provide instructions and time *during* the workshop to complete one or more activities or tasks that will be of value to the participants by the end of the workshop. Play instrumental "working music" while participants complete each activity or task.

Step 5

Continue to invite interaction by asking the audience members to share via chat box what they completed and provide feedback, reinforcement of the lesson, encouragement, and correction when necessary. Use first names of those engaging with you to build "social proof" and rapport with them.

Step 6

Present an offer in line with the content of the workshop. Tell participants what they will receive, how it will help them continue the work from the call, how to get it, and exactly what to do now. Give participants a compelling reason to invest in your offer before the call ends and be sure to provide and explain the details of a guarantee.

Step 7

Answer questions, monitor sales, and welcome by name those who invested in the program. Continue to encourage sales and reinforce the end-of-call deadline.

$ How you make money

Charge admission

Write a sales page and sell admission to your virtual workshop. Participants will pay in advance to join you. In that case, you can choose not to sell anything further during your workshop or you can upsell continued coaching, consulting, or mentoring (see Way 13), a mastermind program, or advanced training.

Upsell from free

Hold the workshop for free and, following the steps above, sell a product or service during the virtual workshop.

Be an affiliate

Be an affiliate for someone else, and allow him or her to introduce the workshop to your community for free. Most will follow a similar format to that described above. You will likely earn 50 percent commission for sending about three email invitations over the course of a week or so, introducing the presenter and sharing a few comments while the presenter does most of the heavy lifting.

Recruit affiliates

Reach out to others who have audiences similar to yours and invite them to be your affiliates and introduce you to their communities. Follow the steps above and give your hosts a generous commission (again, 50 percent is common) for marketing you to their people.

WAY **12**

Host a Telesummit

Think of a telesummit as a live multi-speaker event without the hassle of travel and logistics of hotels and conference rooms. You can present telesummits from the convenience of your home or office, and that convenience extends to your participants and speakers. Because the overhead expenses are so low, it's easy to make money with a telesummit.

The main downside to telesummits is that like any event where you have to wrangle multiple speakers, there is a lot of coordination and it can sometimes feel as if you're herding cats. You can choose to organize everything yourself, or if you're organizationally challenged like me, you can hire someone to handle all the details while you focus on being the hostess with the mostest (or host with the most!).

You can present your telesummit in a variety of formats:

- ✓ Live presentation—no interaction with host or audience

- ✓ Live presentation—with interaction from host and/or audience

- ✓ Live presentation—interview style

- ✓ Recorded presentation—no interaction with host

- ✓ Recorded presentation—with interaction from host

- ✓ Video—with Skype or Oovoo.com to record for free

Of the above formats, I personally prefer those that include interaction with at least the speaker and host. The rest of the decisions about your telesummit hinge on how you want to plan your time and the level of interaction you want with your audience.

If you have never run a telesummit, consider running it live over the course of one work week and asking four guest speakers to join you via bridge line that you share with the audience members. Present the content at the same time each day, with one presenter per day. On Friday, you can be your own guest speaker and present your own content.

With more experience, you can run telesummits with twenty or more speakers, presented over the course of a couple weeks in a variety of creative configurations.

$ How you make money

Sell tickets

Sell virtual tickets to the event via a sales page hosted on a website dedicated to the event.

Free admission

Allow audience members to attend the live portion of the event for free and upsell audios only, transcripts only, or both audios and transcripts bundled together. If you provide physical transcripts, CDs, DVDs, and more, you can charge more to cover your physical costs (see Way 15).

Affiliate for your guests

Invite guest speakers to offer products for sale during their presentations and collect an affiliate commission for any sales they make to your community. Guest speakers will usually speak for free if you provide a large, target audience and allow them to sell or provide a gift that will lead to a sale. Also have guest speakers provide an affiliate link so you can follow up after their presentations, offering their products and services to your attendees and the community.

Coaching on
the Phone

When I was a teenager, my dad always used to joke that if I could make money talking on the phone when I grew up, one day I'd be rich. Dad wasn't far off the mark!

You have a number of moneymaking options while speaking to clients on the phone. You could also do the same in person if you have a location and people willing to meet you face to face, either locally or with travel.

To avoid confusion, I'd like to explain the differences, as I understand them, between coaching, consulting, and mentoring:

Coaching involves the coach asking questions and eliciting answers from the client. Coaching is a useful tool for goal setting, creating action steps, and helping you move forward. However, in its purest sense coaching does not involve giving advice or telling a client what to do, but rather allows the client to form his or her own ideas, and you as a coach help your client decide to act on those ideas and plan how they will do so.

Consulting is where you pay a person for his or her expertise in a particular subject area. When my clients hire me to consult with them on public speaking, for example, I share with them what I know based on my background, knowledge, and experience, and I provide strategies, tools, and techniques to use.

Mentoring is a situation where clients decide to work with you because you have achieved something that they would also like to achieve. The mentor's role is to guide, share best practices, give advice, and help direct the "mentee" to move forward toward a desired result.

When all three of these roles are combined, clients often get a customized plan developed with guidance and support from you, along with the skills to achieve their goals and follow through on their plans. Often you will see the terms used interchangeably or simply called "coaching." In this Way, I'll use the word "coaching," but you can use the language that is right for your business and your clients.

Here are the types of coaching you can deliver and make money with:

Private one-to-one, one-off coaching—you and your client on the phone, delivered one time.

Private one-to-one, extended coaching—you and your client on the phone, delivered periodically and usually regularly over a specific amount of time. For example, three months, six months, or a year.

Group one-off coaching—you and a group of clients on the phone, delivered one time. For example, a one-time question and answer call.

Group extended coaching—you and a group of clients on the phone, delivered periodically and usually regularly over a specific amount of time. For example, three months, six months, or a year. Good examples of this coaching type are membership or mastermind groups.

$ How You Make Money

Combination

Sell your preferred type of coaching and/or combine it with any of the other types. For example, perhaps mastermind members get one monthly group call and one monthly thirty-minute private session with you.

Bonus

Use coaching as a bonus incentive for other purchases such as in Ways 4, 10, and 11.

WAY 14

Conduct Phone Interviews

When you conduct and present an effective inter-view with a recognized or emerging expert, you gain several benefits, including relationships with other recognized experts, more exposure to the expert's community, and greater credibility as the go-to person in your area of expertise.

You only need two tools to conduct an interview: a phone and a bridge line with recording capability so you can capture the brilliance of your interviewee. A nice extra to add is a hands-free headset attached to your phone for comfort.

Here are some of the best places to find experts to interview:

Your personal and professional networks

Start asking those you know from your community of friends and business acquaintances for referrals to experts.

Social networking

Ask your online network of friends on Twitter, Facebook, LinkedIn, and wherever else you hang out online whom they know that meets your criteria.

Search engines

Type some keywords for the type of person you are looking for into your favorite search engine. Those who appear on the first page or two of the search results have done some work to reach those spots. Visit their sites to learn more about them and to see if they could be a perfect fit for your project. Send an e-mail introducing yourself, and extend an interview invitation.

Article databases

Experts write and submit articles to high-traffic sites like EzineArticles.com, Ideamarketers.com, LadyPens.com and literally hundreds of other sites. Search those sites for articles related to your topic of interest. Follow the links to the authors' websites and connect with the author if you feel he or she would be a good fit.

Your e-mail inbox

You may already be subscribed to some newsletters by experts who would be perfect for your audience. Hit reply to one of those messages so the sender knows you are already a fan and follower of his or her work.

When determining what questions to ask, your guest may already have a list of questions he or she would feel comfortable answering. However, in your audience's best interests, it's better if you research your own questions that will provide information that's important to your audience. Often you can tweak the questions supplied by the interviewee and add your own to customize the interview for your audience.

$ How You Make Money

Bonus incentive

Use a recording of an expert interview as a bonus for a product you are selling to help "sweeten the pot" for your prospects. That interview could be the determining factor in someone's purchase decision.

Sell a bundle

Conduct several interviews and sell them in one bundled package. Call it "The Definitive Guide to [fill in the blank with your niche's greatest want]."

Build your list

Give the interview recording(s) away as an incentive to build your list of subscribers. Make money on the "back end" through links to your products and services within the auto-responder series as you follow up after the interview giveaway.

Sell a membership

Create a membership program that features interviews with experts as one of the main benefits. Interview one or two experts per month and upload the recordings to the membership site or send them directly to the members.

Resources in this Way:

 Twitter.com

 Facebook.com

LinkedIn.com

 EzineArticles.com

 IdeaMarketers.com

LadyPens.com

WAY 15

Create a Product

Throughout this little book, you have a number of choices when it comes to the types of products you can make with your voice. In fact, see Ways 8, 9, 10, 11, 12, and 14 for more on the various types of speaking you can turn into products. Each of those Ways repurposes content that you originally created at a live workshop, in a webinar, or doing an interview.

Beyond repurposing, however, you could also set out to create a product with your voice that begins as the product you intend, rather than simply re-using what you already created. (And you should definitely be re-using and repurposing the content you already created to bring in more money even after the initial event ends or purpose is fulfilled!)

Here are a few ways to create a product using your voice:

Audio only

Download free audio recording and editing software such as Audacity from Sourceforge.net. Pick up a head set with microphone or a stand-alone microphone that connects via USB cable to your computer. Make your plan, fire up your equipment, and talk!

PowerPoint videos with narration

The PowerPoint 2010 program has the capability to not only create slides, but also to record your voice to narrate the slides. Put together your slide presentation, plug in your USB microphone or headset, and simply speak as you would in front of a live audience. When you're finished, go to "save and send" in the file menu, then "create a video."

Screen capture video with narration

Using screen capture software such as Camtasia, you turn on the software, plug in your USB microphone or headset and talk as you move around various websites. For step-by-step instruction on using Camtasia, see LearnCamtasia.com/webinar/felicia.

"Talking head" video

Digital video cameras have evolved and are now so simple to use, anyone can make a good-quality video where you appear on screen as the star. Audio and lighting are important considerations when creating a product you plan to sell. Consult a professional for more information or hire a videographer to do the technical work for you.

After your content is created, you need to determine the best way to deliver your product. Of course, online digital delivery is popular because of the minimal costs involved. All you really need are PDF files of any written material and online downloadable audios in MP3 format. You can create a hidden digital download page on your website that you only supply to customers, or have a more secure environment such as a password protected membership page to deliver your content.

Also consider offering a physical version of your product. According to a survey conducted by the Glazer-Kennedy organization during the summer of 2011, a full 50 percent of respondents said they would not purchase a product unless it was available in a physical form. That could mean you're losing half your sales!

When planning a physical product delivery you need to consider the following:

✓ Have transcripts made of all audios and videos. My favorite transcript service is PatelEnterprise. net (ask for Minesh).

✓ Get the audios burned onto CD or saved on a customizable MP3 player.

✓ Have videos made into DVDs.

✓ Print manuals, checklists, and other written material.

✓ Create graphics for all CDs, DVDs, packaging, and printed materials.

Remember to figure in packaging, fulfillment, and shipping expenses. For CDs, DVDs, printed pieces, fulfillment, and more, I highly recommend Disk.com as a one-stop shop (ask for Joe).

Resources in this Way:

 Patel Enterprise.net

 Disk.com

Glazer Kennedy Insider's Circle
FeliciaSlattery.com/GKIC

 PowerPoint to Video Tips
FeliciaSlattery.com/PPTvideo

WAY **16**

Voice Overs

Paul Connelly, a vice president with Cisco Corporation, said at a forum in September 2010, "Our stake in the ground is that global traffic will quadruple by 2014, and we believe 90 percent of consumer traffic will be video based." With the proliferation of online video projected to continue growing at an explosive rate, more and more organizations will be jumping to create their own video content for consumers.

Those groups need a voice. That voice can be yours!

Most large corporations have the budget to hire a professional voice over artist for all their projects. If you want to become serious about making money with voice overs, visit the Society of Accredited Voice

Over Artists at SaVoa.org, or unions such as AFTRA. org, SAG.org, ACTRA.ca, or Equity.org.uk.

However, many smaller businesses have tight budgets and may not be able to hire an accredited and union-backed voice over artist. If you have a clear voice and are willing to invest in better-than-average equipment or begin a professional relationship with someone who does, you can make money specializing in voice overs for online videos.

Since YouTube.com started its free video sharing service in April 2005, businesses have been using it for marketing to drive traffic to their sites, build brand awareness, share short snippets of content, and more. Your voice could become the voice of a company.

Here are some ways smaller businesses and organizations may use a voice over:

✓ **Content audios and videos**—reading articles, narrating a PowerPoint video, etc.

✓ **Promotional videos**—used to drive traffic or sell a product

✓ **Welcome videos**—videos welcoming visitors to a website

✓ **Training videos**—a voice to make a video training product, as discussed in Way 14, come to life

✓ **Demo videos**—a showcase for professional speakers, videographers, bands, and entertainers of all kinds

✓ **Outgoing telephone greeting**—Get creative! Many small and home-based business owners want to project an image of professionalism. One way they can do this is by hiring an outside voice to deliver the outgoing message greeting on their phone's voicemail system.

$ How you make money

Market yourself

Market yourself to small businesses with ideas on how they could use your voice over talents and services.

Build partnerships

Partner with professional videographers and have professional-quality recording, editing equipment, and facilities. When one of your partners needs your voice for a project, you make money.

Resources in this Way:

 Society of Accredited Voice Over Artists (SaVOA)
SaVOA.org

 American Federation of Television and Radio Artists (AFTRA)
AFTRA.org

 Screen Actors Guild (SAG)
SAG.org

 Alliance of Canadian Cinema, Television and Radio Artists
ACTRA.org

 Equity
Equity.org.uk

 YouTube.com

Cruise Ship Speaking

And now for a musical interlude:

"Love, exciting and new. Come aboard. We're expecting youuuuuu…. The Love Boat…."

Remember that fun show that aired from 1977–1986? If you recall, *The Love Boat's* cruise director Julie McCoy's job was to make sure the passengers enjoyed their stay onboard. As a cruise ship speaker, you could enjoy that job, too!

There are a couple of ways to be a speaker on board a cruise ship. One is to be hired directly by the cruise company and the other is to host your own event on a ship.

Be hired

If you want to be hired by the cruise companies, it's good if you first know the lingo. Cruise companies use terms like enrichment series, adult enrichment, and onboard enrichment programs to describe the speakers aboard their ships.

While there are a number of cruise companies that offer onboard enrichment opportunities for their passengers, Daniel Hall, the leading authority on cruise ship speaking, recommends the cruise lines Royal Caribbean International and Princess Cruises (of the aforementioned *Love Boat* fame!) for beginners to the cruise ship speaking world.

When you are hired to speak on a cruise ship, you present a specified number of lectures or seminars on a ship's days at sea—the days the ship is not in port—while passengers are essentially "stuck" onboard (if you could call all the food you can eat, entertainment on every deck, and fun galore "stuck"). Often lectures run about 45 to 50 minutes, and are both informative and entertaining.

At the end of the cruise the passengers will rate you on not only your presentation, but also your demeanor throughout the cruise. Speakers who receive the best ratings are often welcomed back with open arms.

You can choose to contact the cruise companies directly or work with an agency that specializes in booking onboard entertainment.

Host your own event

If you're interested in cruising, you've undoubtedly heard about the various special interest types of cruises, such as radio station–sponsored cruises, hobby groups, religious groups, and more. You, too, can host your own cruise with special activities and events for your guests.

By far the easiest way to do this is to connect with a travel agent who specializes in creating cruise events. The travel agency has relationships with cruise companies and will set you up with special cocktail receptions, meeting rooms onboard, and even off-ship excursions at the various ports. Then plan your event according to the ideas suggested in Way 9.

$ How You Make Money

You should know when the cruise ships hire you directly your payment is in the form of a free cruise for you and a guest. As such, this is not a way to make money, but a way for you to save money on a fabulous vacation. Cruises usually cost thousands of dollars, and you get it for free! You are responsible for your travel expenses to and from the port where the ship sets sail and docks upon return.

One way you can make money if the ships hire you directly is to sell your books, CDs, or DVDs at the back of the room if that is acceptable with cruise line. Always check your contract and rules for speakers to be certain.

To make the most money as a cruise ship speaker, host your own event. For every fifteen cabins your group books, you get one cabin free of charge, so you only have to sell fifteen seats to your event. Then, in addition to the cruise fees, your participants pay for the event. You can bundle the ticket price for the cruise and your event together, and also offer a "cruise only" ticket for friends, partners, or spouses.

Resources in this Way:

 Cruise Ship Speaking
FeliciaSlattery.com/speakoncruises

Teach a Class at Your Park District

Park districts offer far more than kids' swimming lessons and aerobics classes for moms. In the most recent catalog from my own park district, I counted fifty-two classes and programs for adults—not including fitness classes. A small selection of classes offered by my park district include Classic Drawing with Colored Pencils, Wildlife Photography in Your Backyard, Beer Brewing 101, Computer Tips and Tricks, General Automotive Maintenance, Dog Obedience: End the Leaps and Bounds (ooohh I might have to sign up my new dog Sadie for that one!), Vegetarian Lifestyles, Grocery Guru, Metabolism Makeover, and Cooking for Couples: The Power of Chocolate.

With topics as varied as those at just my small park district alone, that, my friend, is the sound of opportunity knocking for a speaker!

This is one Way I used myself in the early phases of starting my business. What's so great about teaching a class through the park district? Many reasons! It's close to home, so no travel expenses and free parking! Your name is listed in the catalog as the instructor, leading to more publicity and visibility for you and more credibility as the go-to person in your community. In addition, students can become private coaching clients (see Way 13) or be interested in attending a longer workshop (Way 9), webinar (Way 10), or seminar (Way 11). You can even use the content from your Signature Speech (Way 21) for a class with little effort. And finally, the park district does the marketing and fills the seats for you.

Guidelines for your park district class:

Plan on the group being relatively small, as most park districts do not have facilities to accommodate large sit-down lecture classes.

Conduct activities that encourage interaction between you and the participants.

If you plan to use PowerPoint or other electronics, bring your own equipment, including laptop, projector, screen, and anything else you may need. Park district facilities are usually limited (I taught my class in a preschool classroom in the evening).

Activities that work well include planning sheets, journaling exercises, quizzes, assessments, group discussions, showing examples from TV or movies (if the technology is available to show them), case studies, and writing assignments.

$ How You Make Money

Each park district will vary, but at my park district, I set the dates and times, the length, and the fee for the course. I submitted an invoice after the course ended and earned 80 percent of the total class fees paid by participants.

WAY 19

Get a Sponsor

One of the biggest myths about sponsorships is they are only available to nonprofit groups, associations, and little leagues. Yet sponsors want to put their products and services in front of their ideal target market just as we do. According to Shannon Cherry, creator of the *Sponsorship Made Simple Academy* at GetSponsoredLikeFelicia.com, sponsoring is a viable marketing tool. Organizations can often get a better return on their investment through sponsorships than with traditional advertising.

When a sponsor decides to support you, they are introduced to your community (subscribers, social media followers, newsletter readers, etc.) and they receive your endorsement, which savvy sponsors know will go a long way in getting them new customers.

There are specific requirements a sponsor will look for. These include: a good match to their ideal market—you should be able to deliver an audience that a sponsor wants to reach—and a large and responsive reach. Remember to include all your numbers such as your newsletter lists, social media following, local groups, numbers of attendees at events, and more. You should also offer a business to build a lasting relationship with—they don't want a fly-by-night flash in the pan—and a specific plan for their organization to reach your audience creatively.

Things sponsors invest in:

✓ A live or virtual event that you host (see Ways 8, 9, 10, 11, 12, 14, and 15)

✓ A live or virtual event where you are a guest speaker (see Ways 1, 2, and 4)

✓ Your attendance at a conference or event (yes even if you're not speaking!)

✓ A blog post, Tweet, or Facebook status update

✓ Your website

✓ Giveaway promotional items

✓ Contests that you hold or organize

- ✓ Videos or products (digital or physical) that you produce

- ✓ Your printed newsletter or digital ezine

- ✓ Your book, if you self-publish

$ How You Make Money

There are two types of sponsorship support available:

Cash

Obviously this is where you bring in actual money. Shannon Cherry teaches how to calculate the amount of sponsorship money you should request in your sponsorship proposal, also known as your sponsorship deck.

In-kind gifts

While in-kind gifts are not technically cash, they do represent cash in your pocket because you are getting something of value to you, which you might have otherwise purchased.

Resources in this Way:

 GetSponsoredLikeFelicia.com

WAY 20

Speak at Colleges

In the spring of 2011, Nicole "Snooki" Polizzi of reality television fame was paid $32,000 to deliver a presentation to the students at Rutgers University in New Jersey, where she talked about the pouf in her hair, fist pumps, and the lifestyle she has described as "GTL —gym, tanning, laundry." Nobel Prize–winning novelist Toni Morrison was paid $30,000 to speak at the same institution's commencement address in May 2011. (Don't get me started on why Snooki got more . . .) Add it up and that's $62,000 for just two speakers at one college.

There is money in the college speaking market, even if you're not willing to appear on TV as a drunken, boy-crazy fool or don't happen to have a Nobel Prize in your back pocket. In fact, you can often garner speaking fees in the $2,000–$5,000 range, plus expenses, if you have a topic that is of interest to the college market.

Having taught at colleges and universities all over the Chicago area for more than a decade after working in an enrollment department, I have a unique perspective on the college speaking market. Here are some popular topics for college market speaking:

College success

Succeeding in college includes test-taking strategies, choosing a major for a lifelong passion, how to build your personal brand early, time-management strategies, learning and memory programs, and speed-reading.

Student life

Succeeding in student life can include fraternity/sorority life; dating, sex and relationships; alcohol and drug awareness; mental health issues and wellness; multiculturalism and diversity issues; and parent, sibling and alumni programs.

Success after college

Speaking about succeeding after college includes how to get a job after graduation, how to write a resume that sells, the pitfalls of social media during the job hunt, money and finance, and business and entrepreneurship.

Entertainment

Anything funny or entertaining that is appropriate for traditional-age college students.

To get into the college speaking market, contact the campus activities office at the school where you wish to speak. There is a trade journal called *Campus Activities Programming*, published by the National Association for Campus Activities, which you can access and read for free online through NACA.org. If this is a market you want to pursue, consider advertising in this publication and networking with its members.

Another campus speaking option is to connect with the adult enrichment and professional development centers at community colleges and universities about teaching non-credit courses.

Finally, if you have a master's degree or higher, you could apply to teach a for-credit course. In this case, you would be an adjunct faculty member with all of the joys of teaching and none of the hassles of full-time academic employment.

$ How You Make Money

Most paid campus speakers fall into the Keynote Speaker category (see Way 1).

Non-credit course instructors earn from hundreds up to the low thousands of dollars, depending on the course length, content, and school policies.

Adjunct faculty earn anywhere on the low end from $1,200 per fifteen-week semester to $5,000 or more. Typically the larger the school and the more public funds available, the higher the salary is for all faculty members. Large universities with the former "Research I" designation have the deepest pockets. Small liberal arts private schools tend to have the smallest budgets, followed by community colleges.

Resources in this Way:

 National Association for Campus Activities (NACA)
NACA.org

Signature Speech™ Solution

Since I created the Signature Speech™ in 2007, I have successfully used this technique personally (and still do) and have taught it to thousands of business professionals around the world over the years.

Do not be confused. The Signature Speech™ is not the "elevator speech" you're supposed to spit at someone when they ask you, "What do you do?" (Ugh don't get me started—that's a whole 'nother book!). Rather, the Signature Speech™ is a persuasive presentation you deliver, usually for free, to a live audience filled with your ideal target market as a tool specifically to market your business, begin new relationships, and generate more cash flow both immediately and for the long term.

You can deliver your Signature Speech™ locally in your community (see Ways 6 and 8), virtually (see Ways 10, 11, and 12), or slightly reconfigure your speech and deliver it as an interview on a radio program where you are the guest (see Way 14).

Here are eight steps to get started with using a Signature Speech™ to market your business and be successful with this powerful marketing technique:

Step 1

Determine your topic. As an expert you've got something to share with the world. Determine what exactly you believe audiences want to hear about.

Step 2

Do your research. Often you won't have to look much beyond your own bookshelf, but you have to fill your speech with great content and share where that information came from.

Step 3

Write your speech. Your speech should lead your audience in the direction of your main purpose, which is to be able to connect with them later. Provide them with useful details that make your audience members salivate to provide you with their information.

Step 4

Get booked to deliver your speech. Think of places where your ideal audience gets together on a regular basis. Service organizations like Rotary International or Lions Club? Moms' groups? Share the benefits your audience will walk away with and you're in.

Step 5

Practice your speech. Stand up and practice out loud—not in your head, or in the car, or murmuring in front of your computer screen. The more you practice, the more confident you will feel.

Step 6

Deliver the speech. Remember this golden rule of speaking: It's always about your audience. Feeling nervous? Just make sure you're giving your audience the best you can in that very moment. I call it "serving from the stage."

Step 7

Follow up. Have people in the audience given you their business cards? Did people ask you questions? Make sure you follow up with those who expressed an interest and do it as soon as possible upon arriving back at your office.

Step 8

Keep in touch. Use direct mail via newsletters, mobile marketing, or send an electronic newsletter or ezine. (Mine is called *Creating Connections* and is delivered every other Wednesday afternoon.) Your job now is to stay top of mind for those who saw you because your speech was only the beginning of your relationship with them.

There is so much more to this Way. In fact I have a full six-module training with approximately twenty-five hours of audio and video content, reams of written steps, checklists, templates, examples, and more at SignatureSpeech.com. However, for more information on how to get started, download the free MP3 at SignatureSpeechSecrets.com.

$ How You Make Money

In order to maximize your financial results from delivering your Signature Speech™ for free, do the following:

Sell from the stage

Sell your books, a product, or service on the spot. See Ways 3, 4, and 5 for more.

Meet and greet

Take the time to shake hands with everyone waiting in line to speak with you.

Collect contact info

Get business cards from everyone you meet and speak with personally. Send those people a special follow-up greeting after your speech so they know you remember them. Call them directly or send a handwritten note. Direct mail is making a comeback as a follow-up strategy. Don't you love getting "real" mail that's not a bill? I use the system at CardsFromFelicia.com.

Offer a consultation

Call those who have detailed questions. These are the people who are telling you, "I want to know more!" If they have detailed questions, they may want to engage with you privately.

Follow up right away

Get the contact information of everyone in the audience and permission to send more free information. It can be a special report, an article, an e-course, a video or audio recording, or even a resource list. Use your auto-responder service to do the heavy lifting and create a series of messages designed to offer more products and services for sale and show how people can access them. I use and highly recommend SimpleSpeakingFollowUp.com.

Resources in this Way:

 SignatureSpeechSecrets.com

 CardsFromFelicia.com

 SimpleSpeakingFollowUp.com

About the Author

Felicia J. Slattery, M.A., M.Ad.Ed., is a professional speaker, communication consultant, and speaker trainer based in the Chicago area and has made a comfortable living using a combination of most of the 21 Ways in this book. You can learn more about her at 21WaysToMakeMoneySpeaking.com

 21WaystoMakeMoneySpeaking.com

Start Making Money Speaking with Just 1 Speech Strategy!

With most of the 21 Ways to Make Money Speaking, you can start by having just one speech open all the doors for you. It's called your Signature Speech.

I invite you to visit SignatureSpeechSecrets.com to download a 30-minute totally FREE audio recording where you'll discover what YOU can do to take advantage of this amazing and powerful tool to achieve massive success in your business.

After listening to this recording, you'll know exactly what you need to do to get your Signature Speech ready to work for you. And you can start immediately! Soon you'll see results for yourself.

What to do now:

1. Visit SignatureSpeechSecrets.com and enter your first name and primary email address.

2. Click the link in when it arrives in your inbox to verify your email address for your Signature Speech Secrets and more great tips to follow!

3. Listen and get ready to deliver your own Signature Speech!

Got questions?

You've read the book. And now you're excited to make money speaking. Yay you!

If you truly are serious about hanging your shingle as a speaker, let me help you with a "mostly free" 10-minute Speaker Profit Session.

Why mostly free? Well, you'll have to provide your email address and fill out a brief online question-naire to get started. Pretty simple when you consider you'll have 10 minutes privately with someone who is using many of the ways in this book today to make a living with speaking and who consults with others to do the same!

How to claim your free session:

1. Visit
21WaysToMakeMoneySpeaking.com/profitsession

2. Enter your name and primary email address.

3. Click the link in when it arrives in your inbox to verify your email address and to go to the online questionnaire.

4. Complete the online questionnaire, submit your responses and on the next page schedule your appointment at your convenience.

I look forward to "speak" with you soon!

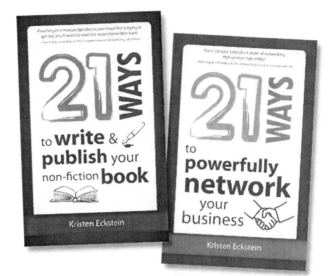

Don't miss a single book in the series!

Look for more *21 Ways*™ books at:

21WaysBooks.com